LONG TERM CARE CLAIM FILING

A Field Guide for Prince(ss) Dutiful Heir

by Dr. Stana Martin

Acknowledgements:

This is my first book.

It would never have seen life had it not been for my sister who came along side me during a dark day and believed in me and my vision of making a difference in the lives of families.

Family.
It may not be all we want it to be – but if we are lucky, family can be what we need it to be. Here's to you, Sis!

TABLE OF CONTENTS

Prince(ss) Dutiful and the Highly Stressful Situation

A Tale Told in One Myth and Four Reality Acts.

So you have found this field guide and are wondering if it will be the answer to your prayers about filing a claim on a long term care insurance policy. The answer is, well maybe. Much will hinge on how quickly you learn and how good you are at following instructions. This guide lays out the main things to know and what to do to have a successful claim – but you may still decide you want to hire professional help when all is said and done because, quite honestly, this insurance isn't like other insurance – it is a horse of a different color altogether! Where other types of insurance have standardized codes and insurance professionals to handle problems, this insurance largely relies on inexperienced family members to process highly idiosyncratic paperwork. Nor is the process always simple or self-evident. To illustrate, let's follow my favorite fairy tale person thru the process .....

One Myth

Once upon a time there was Parent. Parent did really well for a long time, but eventually Parent became Aging Parent and then Aging Parent became Parent-Who-Needs-Help (or, just Parent for short). So as Parent needs more help, Dutiful Heir steps up. It may be Prince Dutiful, but the vast majority of the time it is Princess Dutiful (or Dutiful Daughter-in-Law). For brevity hereafter, we'll just say Dutiful and use the female gender – really, nearly 90% of all direct care today is still done by women, so in this fairy tale, let's just call a frog a frog, shall we?

So on Friday, Aging Parent has to go to the cardiologist (or proctologist or some other -ist). Dutiful makes time in her busy schedule to take Parent to the doctor. At the doctor's office, Dutiful gets Parent's insurance cards and hands them to the Nice Lady behind the window. Nice Lady photocopies them and returns them to Dutiful, who dutifully tucks them back into Parent's wallet. Then Dutiful and Parent go back, see the doc, and as they exit, Another Nice Lady says something like, "No money due today. We will bill the insurance and we'll let you know if you owe anything."

Dutiful nods absently because her mind has already spun to the next to-do item on today's list as she lovingly helps Parent out to the car. Off they go into the sunset. The whole process in Dutiful's mind looks like this:

One Myth

Dutiful's sole responsibility in this was carting the insurance cards to the window and back to the wallet. Parent had even less. What Dutiful and Parent have forgotten – if they ever knew – is that behind the window where Nice Lady sat, was a Small Army of People whose ONLY job is medical records management and insurance claim filing. The reason it is so easy for Dutiful is because the doctor is paying the Small Army to wrangle the claim process.[1] Further, Small Army are all professionals in the insurance and medical records industry, many of them with one or more years of formal training.

Does this work in long term care insurance? Not hardly. First, long term care insurance benefits are rarely assigned (see foot note), so the long term care provider has low incentive to wrangle the claim successfully.

1 The doctor is willing to do this because Parent has "assigned benefits" to the doctor. This means the insurance company is going to pay the doctor directly. So the doctor now has a vested financial interest in getting the insurance to pay correctly – s/he is highly motivated and willing to pay Nice Lady and Another Nice Lady as well as Small Army.

Secondly, medical insurance has a standardized coding and billing system in place (called ICD-9 or ICD-10 codes) - long term care insurance does not. Thus, most long term care providers do not want to take on claim filing in the same way that doctors or hospitals do because each claim requires individualized attention and idiosyncratic adjustments. Further, there is no "Small Army" of staff - there is usually just one Nice Lady who has limited to no formal training.

So who files the claim paperwork in long term care insurance? Dutiful does. Princess Dutiful who is working a full time job typically, has grown children and possibly grandchildren of her own, a spouse or partner, and volunteer work on weekends - Dutiful who is actually a teacher (or banker or any other profession - but not an insurance professional) and has no expertise in insurance language or insurance procedures. Dutiful, who is only one person and not an army of people, is now the one who will be responsible to file the claim and make sure it pays correctly. This Myth has set Dutiful up for a very big fall. Let us name it "A Very Stressful Situation" and lay out the ins-and-outs of this Very Stressful Situation in Four Acts. So, onwards our fairy tale rambles to reveal The REAL story of how claims work in long term care insurance.

Act One

Dutiful takes the policy to the long term care provider.

So far everything looks normal to Dutiful. Parent is now receiving care from a Home Health Care provider or Assisted Living Facility or Nursing Home (let's just use ALF to make it simple). And since the ALF is the care provider, Dutiful brings the insurance policy to the ALF just like she did the Medicare cards to the cardiologist. The Nice Lady at the ALF, having been here before, says "OK. We can help you with this." And Dutiful thinks (oh let me emphasize THINKS!) that all is well and good just as it was every other time she had insurance for Parent.

Act Two

The long term care provider initiates the claim.

Good ALF administrators (or HHC or NH) will take the policy, find the 800# and call the carrier to indicate that a claim needs to be opened. The carriers will (sometimes) talk to them. IF the carrier will talk to the ALF administrator, the administrator can get a copy of the required claim form. If not, the forms will all be mailed to the address on file for the policy.

Here is the first error in our comedy of errors. No one thought to change the address on file, so all this very important paperwork is mailed to Parent's address on Mulberry Ln, but Parent now lives in Harmony Gardens ALF at the other end of town. At this point, the process looks something like this where the lines indicate communication – either paperwork or phone calls (please note, Parent has almost dropped from the equation altogether!):

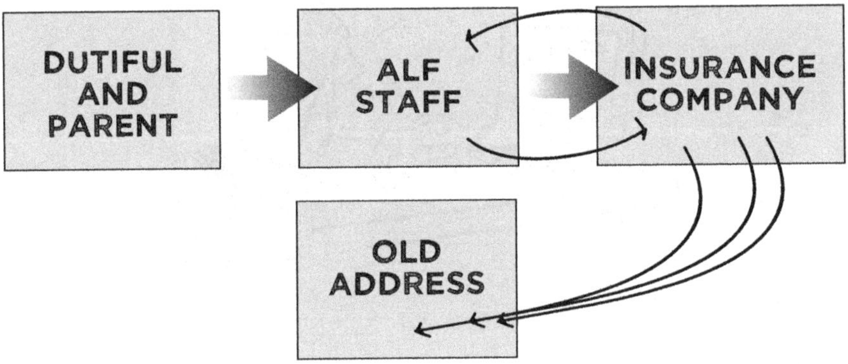

Act Three

More records requested.

Dutiful eventually – FINALLY -- discovers these important papers in the pile of mail at Parent's house. She gets the claim form over to the ALF and the Nice Lady fills it out and sends it in. But we are still not home free. This triggers new requests for information including but not limited to:

- doctor's notes and/or
- orders for care
- clinical test results
- licensures
- assessments
- plan of care
- daily visitation notes
- admission and discharge notes from the hospital
- admission and discharge notes from the rehab

In short, the carrier has the right (and responsibility to stock holders) to require enough documentation to prove there is a legitimate claim and no fraud. The carrier is looking for evidence of (1) proof of medical need for care and (2) a care giver that meets the contract specifications in the policy.

The process now looks like this:

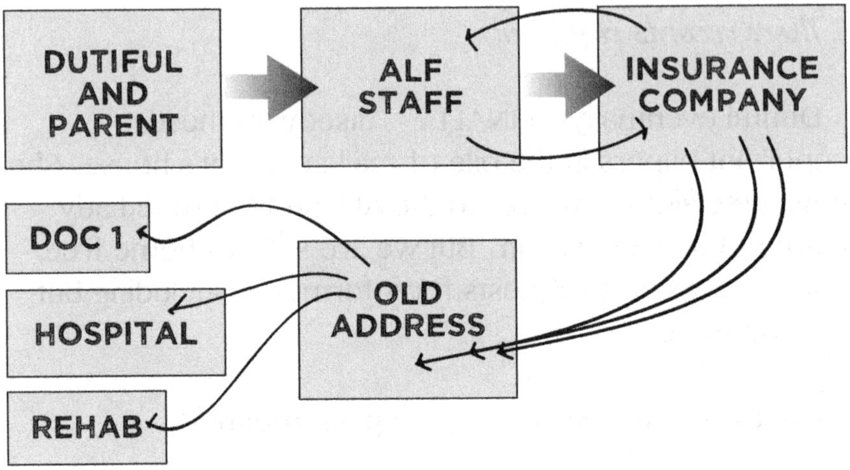

Dutiful is beginning to see that this is NOT like all the other times s/he has helped Parent. This time is markedly different. If this were a Greek tragedy, now would enter the Chorus to wail and weep cueing the audience to the emotional plot! As with every other fairy tale, there comes the moment when all looks lost and we wonder if the hero(ine) is going to come out on top. We are now, my dears, approaching that moment!

Act Four

Death by Document.

So now Dutiful has spent several hours reading everything. She has also called the carrier (mayhap more than once to ask questions and to sort out vocabulary that she didn't know or understand). She has managed to make a comprehensive list of which document needs to go to which care provider and has a notebook where she is tracking what is missing and what has yet to be delivered to the carrier for documentation. NOW, Dutiful runs the requests for forms to be filled out and documents around to all the right places. But we still are not at the end because EACH of these entities must also RETURN all the documents to the carrier. And sometimes these are not small amounts of records – one recent fax at our office from a rehab unit was 75 pages! Imagine if the fax machine broke midway through, or smeared on page 47.

You see, Dutiful is still at the mercy of other people doing their jobs well and following up to be sure that everything is done, done right, and that no technical glitch threw a gremlin into the process. But Dutiful, not knowing this is the process, assumes that – because she dropped off the required forms at the various places – that these will all get done in a timely manner, AND that they will get to the carrier in their entirety. The Very Stressful Situation is, in the meantime, becoming more stressful because all this time Dutiful has been paying for Parent's care from Parent's dwindling resources. By this point Dutiful *really* wants the policy to kick in and start picking up some of the cost.

Insert more Greek Choirs moaning and wringing their hands... As good as our medical system is, medical records are still not 100% digitized or even full proof in accuracy. The chance of some medical records failure causing problems with the claim approval is still high. We must add to this technical problem a human problem: most doctors have never read a long term care policy. Since there are no standardized codes they can use, the doctor really has no idea what s/he should be writing in the records to prove claim validity. Given the technical and human potential for error, it is more of a wonder that claims are ever approved rather than the more common cry of "why aren't they approved"?!

So our long-suffering hero(ine) is still not out of the woods. Someone (usually Dutiful), must follow up on each of these additional records needed and be sure everything gets to the carrier without a glitch. This can be a near-nightmare level of stress if there is more than one doctor or hospital or rehab. It is not uncommon for Parent to be in home care for osteoporosis frailty and one day fall and break a hip... or have a small stroke. So we could find a situation where – right in the middle of trying to get the claim approved – parent went to Hospital A and then Rehab A... where they had a little slip, fell and broke a hip so back to Hospital B this time and then Rehab B. This means that Dutiful must chase records from BOTH hospitals and BOTH rehabs and ALL relevant doctors to have properly submitted documentation.

Finally, our fairytale would not be complete without introducing The Independent Assessor – a person who is assigned by the carrier to come do a face-to-face visit with Parent. Put yourself in Parent's shoes for just a second... a complete stranger is coming to ask you if you can toilet and handle your own hygiene (for one – there are many such embarrassing questions). Which of us would say, "No. Can't do that on my own – need someone to do it for me."? Most humans – clinging to what shreds of dignity they have left – put their best foot forward and try to seem at least somewhat competent. This is one time, however, when Parent MUST admit to needing help. If Parent does a "best foot forward lie" to the Assessor, then you won't get a claim approved.

So here, at the end of Act 4 (Death By Document) is the entire process:

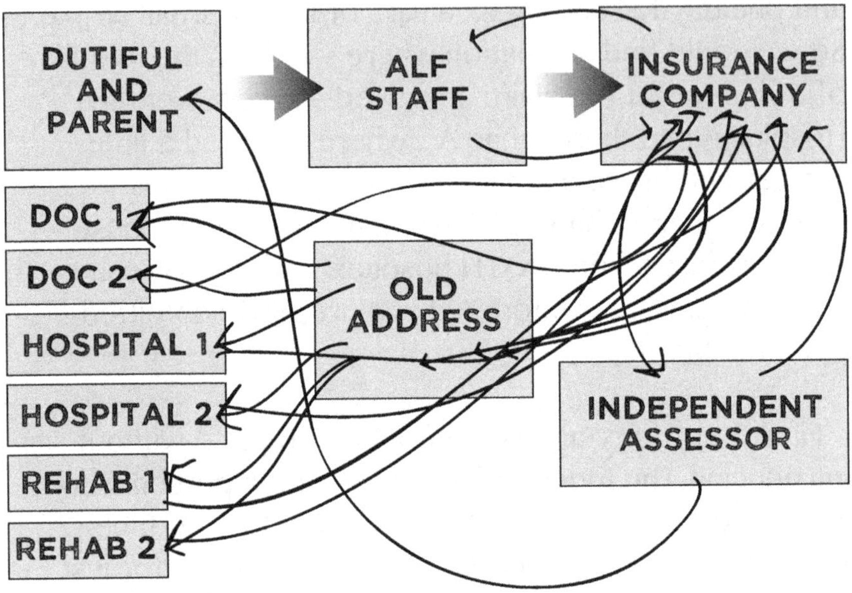

In the world of medical insurance – you know where Dutiful took Parent to the cardiologist? – it is easy-peasy for Dutiful to be, well, dutiful. The long term care claim process is much more fraught with complexity and opportunities for things to just go plain wrong!

To be fair, some carriers are more committed to helping family manage this process than others. Some carriers will actually contact the doctors, hospitals, rehabs, and care providers directly on behalf of the claimant once a claim is requested or opened. While this relieves Dutiful of the frightful mess of it all, it comes with its own set of potential missteps which we will discuss in the next section.[2] The bottom of it all is that what Dutiful THOUGHT was going to happen simply does not happen – the process is complex (no more so than other insurance, mind) and someone has to manage it (just like the Small Army at the doctor's office). But unlike health insurance, Dutiful cannot completely rely on the Nice Lady at the ALF (NH, HHC, or other!) to manage the process. That person is not a Small Army – s/he will only be able to manage a small portion of the process.

2 This is a problem we call "precision matching" and discuss in depth later in this Field Guide.

We now come to the end of our One Myth and Four Acts fairy tale. Poor Dutiful Heir! His/Her life has revolved around a Very Stressful Situation because s/he is coping with the care decisions and needs of Parent while also trying to manage his/her own house, job, family, and finances. In essence, Dutiful has taken on TWO houses to run: her own and Parent's. If you are feeling exhausted, worn to a frazzle, and just want to pitch it all in... well you are not alone. All the Dutifuls are in the same boat with you. The long term care claim can – sometimes – be managed within this chaos. But often, if there is only one Dutiful Heir, it simply becomes too much to bear up under. If anything is going to be tossed overboard, it will be the long term care claim because the other things are far more immediate in terms of need.

There really is a happy ending for Dutiful Heir. There are ways of handling this process that aren't quite as maddening as the haphazard way it normally rolls out. The rest of this Field Guide will lay out in detail what needs to be done.

But in broad brushstrokes, Dutiful will need to:

1) Read the contract

2) Maintain a Contact Log

3) Follow up consistently with every player at the table.

Forewarned really is forearmed. A long term care policy is a powerful tool in helping families cope with the high costs of care. But like any tool designed to cut through difficult or painful parts of life, it needs to be used wisely and handled with care. Around here we have seen a long term care policy be THE tool that cuts through 80% of the stress in the Highly Stressful Situation. In fact, for the rest of this guide, we are going to show you how to transform this tool that could cut in any direction to make it a sword worthy of its name.[3]

There is but one word of caution before we launch full scale into the rest of the field guide: vocabulary... This industry, no less than any others, is jargon heavy and runs on an alphabet soup of short hand. We will make every effort to define terms as we move along. However, in the interest of clarity we have provided a shortened dictionary at the end of this guide. A more comprehensive dictionary of terms can be found in the document produce by the National Association of Insurance Commissioners (NAIC) titled *Long Term Care Insurance Buyer's Guide*. It is generally downloadable from the State Insurance Commissioner's site for your state – and if not there you can find a version thru the NAIC's website directly. Further, and perhaps most importantly, it is updated each year.

With that last cautionary word in hand, let us now, dutiful one, dive into the deep waters of long term care contracts.

---

3 No one can guarantee that a claim will be approved in advance of submission of all forms to the carrier. To date, the carrier is the arbiter of approval on a claim. The burden of proof for claim eligibility lies with the claimant. It is precisely this grey area where attorneys are sometimes called upon to pursue legal recourse. Clearly there is potential conflict of interest if the carrier – who has an apparent financial incentive to NOT approve claims – is the final arbiter of whether a claim is approved or not. Generally we have found most carriers pay well once all documentation is correct and matches the contract. Nevertheless, the basic question remains.

The Contract

Reading the contract first requires that you have a copy of the contract. Even after having done this for a number of years, I am still amazed at the condition in which long term care contracts walk into our office. Generally you will face one of two scenarios:

(1) Mr. or Mrs. Keep Everything – if this is your Parent, you will have an inch or two-inch thick folder of contract, brochures, loose sheets of paper, and various items in an aging and beat up folder or box. It will not be well organized or sorted – just everything jammed into one large receptacle. OR...

(2) You will have found a bank statement where there is a reoccurring charge that says something cryptic like: Carrier LTCi draft monthly premium. Suddenly

NOTE BENE: sometimes carriers will speak with you in the early stages of helping clients without legal authorization, but just as often, they will balk if you are not the policy owner him/herself. One of the first things you will need is legal authority to speak with the carrier about medical and financial details and have this on file with the carrier. This typically comes in the form of a Durable Power of Attorney or at bare minimum a HIPAA release form signed by Parent.

hope springs up in your chest that buried somewhere in Parent's office is a long term care policy.

Your goal in each instance is the same: figure out if there are benefits that can be claimed to off-set the costs of current care. However, your path to that goal may be very different in each case! Scenario #1 is going to require a strong cup of coffee and an hour or so of quiet time to start sorting the various documents in to "useful" and "not useful". You hope eventually to find the policy itself and any addenda that were filed since it was originally purchased. Scenario #2 may require more sleuthing - someone has to identify who the carrier is, get a phone number for them and try to get someone on the phone who can help you discern if there IS a long term care policy (or if it is life, disability or some other type of insurance). If you do find it is a long term care policy, the next step is to request a duplicate copy of the policy (see the *NOTE BENE* box!).

You are, frankly, unarmed unless you have a copy of the policy and can actually READ the details in the contract. Once you have safely negotiated the scrambled pile of papers and/or managed to get a carrier to send a duplicate policy, you can begin the serious business of figuring what the benefits are and if there is a likely claim.

Once you are certain you have a clean and legitimate copy of the contract in hand, you can now start getting answers. Our first recommendation is that you call the carrier to ask questions about what benefits are available in the policy. In a few pages, we will talk about how to read the benefits summary page (also sometimes called the Declaration Page). However, there may be letters of instruction, signed forms, or other things on file with the carrier that modify the original contract. ALWAYS CALL the carrier to confirm available benefits and if anything doesn't square with your read (once we show you how!), ASK for clarification and/or copies of the documents that modified the contract. Remember that, when you call the carrier, you are getting an employee – a human being – that may or may not be making a mistake as they answer your questions. I have never known an employee to deliberately give false information – but humanity shows up on most of us on any given day. So do not hesitate to ask more questions and ask for proof of the assertion if it seems different than what you are reading.

CALLBACK TIP: Call the carrier and ask all your questions. Hang up, call them right back and get an alternate person to answer the phone. Ask your questions again. You are looking for consistency in the answers – if you are getting different answers, this should be a flag that something in the file at the carrier may be incorrect or, more likely, that one of the people you got on the phone provided inaccurate info. Call a third time if the first two don't agree with each other. Play dumb – Call back like you didn't JUST call in! This only works, by the way, if the carrier is large enough to have more than one person. If it is a small carrier with ONLY one person working claims, well, calling back and asking same questions five minutes later won't win you any good will points!

KEEP A CONTACT LOG: This one is an item we just can't emphasize enough [I wanted to put large stars, bold lines, and many exclamation points here so you wouldn't miss this part - my editor wouldn't let me. You must imagine them]... You should start and keep a detailed contact log on the case from the get-go. A good contact log will date/time stamp every phone conversation, email, fax or other communique you engage in when researching a policy or making a claim.

Good information will include the:

- phone, email or fax number
- name of the company contacted
- person's name you communicated with, and
- details of what was done or said.

Carriers - especially larger ones - are recording the calls and making detailed notes in their own contact log on a case. Your contact log can mean the difference between getting the claim approved or not. So, we generally recommend you start this as soon as you know you are the one who is going to wrangle this through to "approved" status.

> ***NOTE BENE:***
> Recorded lines are both training for staff, and a source of legal evidence. Never forget that carriers are (probably) recording your call.

Parts of a Contract:

Contracts can be 10 pages or they can be upwards of 50 pages. Some of that information will be "boiler plate" (i.e. statements that identify which state's laws will take precedence or that the contract is to be understood in its entirety or...) and some of it will be extremely valuable as you run triage on your claim.

The main parts of most contracts are:

1. The policy schedule (sometimes called the "Dec Page" or "Declaration page"),
2. The definitions section,
3. Medical triggers and types of care it pays for,
4. Claim procedures,
5. Any riders or modifiers (this is the one item that may not be part of every contract).

I wish I could tell you that there is a standard order on these key parts but, sadly, not so. With 30+ years of contract variation in the industry, nearly every contract will be different. But you should be able to find all of these parts somewhere in the policy.

1) The Policy Schedule (Dec Page)

This page will lay out the basic benefits that were purchased. There are main benefits and then other benefits you should look for (see Table 1). Because there can be quite a bit of information to track here and because it can be modified by the definitions or riders found later in the contract, we recommend that you have a separate sheet to list these so you can add notes as you find them. A simple spreadsheet often allows you track items, amounts, and any modification notes you run across. Whatever you do, BE SURE you have a good grip on the main benefits as these are the bulk of the value of the policy.

> ***NOTE BENE:*** Long term care benefits MAY be taxable upon payout as income. We always advise you get quality advice from a tax professional. You will need to know if the policy is a Tax-Qualified or Non-Tax-Qualified contract. See the definitions of each in Appendix A.

One last note, there can be tax consequences for long term care benefit payouts. You do need to know if the policy is tax-qualified or not tax-qualified. The contract will specify this, usually in the first page or two of the contract (and sometimes on the declaration page as well).

Table 1:

MAIN BENEFITS[4]	OTHER BENEFITS[5]
• **Benefit amount** (usu-aly listed as an a dollar amount per day, or week or month) • **Total Pool of money** (list-ed as a dollar figure) and / or Time window (listed as days or years) • **Elimination period** abbre-viated EP (listed as days – typical are 0, 20, 30, 45, 90 or 100 or 180). This is the deductible. The client pays the full amount of care for this time and then the policy will begin to pay its portion • Inflation growth (there are many possibilities here – see the definitions given in Appendix A)	• Shared Care • Survivorship • Waiver for HHC (some-times: Waiver of EP for HHC) • Ambulance benefit • Stay At Home Benefit or Home Modification • Restoration • Reduction or increase for ALF (assisted living facility) or HHC • Cash benefits • Rx benefit • Alternate Plan of Care • Bed Reservation Benefit • Respite Care Benefit

4 There is not room here to define each of these terms. Please refer to Appendix for definitions of each item or check with the *Long Term Care Buyer's Guide* mentioned earlier.

5 *Ibid* – see note 3. Further, the list of possible "other" features is much too long to list here. If you find something in the Declaration page that isn't listed here, it will be defined in the contract itself as well in the contract's definition section.

The next pages have examples of Policy Schedule. You will quickly note distinct differences: one is older/simpler and the other is newer/more complicated. Remember these policies have evolved over time in response to the market for services. As the market became more complex, so did the contracts! So it is not surprising that you will find newer policies have more built-in bells and whistles. The main things to know from the Dec page (Policy Schedule) are the top 4: benefit amount, time window or pool of money, deductible, and any inflation compensation. You may want to call the carrier to verify benefits.

PLAY NICE IN THE SANDBOX:

Remember the people who answer phones are human beings... this means they can have bad days, bad attitudes, and bad information - none of which makes them a bad person. Further, that person who answers the phone is not the carrier - so even if you are annoyed with the carrier's procedure, remember the person on the phone is most likely to help if you are polite and can connect in some way besides just-the-facts-jack. The more professional and likeable you are, the more that person is willing to go out of the norm to help get what you need. The employee handles many calls a day – mostly from folks who are not-nice. Play nice in the sand box – you will get farther along and even sometimes earn the benefit of doubt and extra help!

Policy Schedule: Example - 1

POLICY SCHEDULE

NAME OF INSURED:			
COVERED SPOUSE:			
POLICY DATE:	4/22/91	INITIAL PREMIUM:	$118.32
POLICY NUMBER		RENEWAL PREMIUM:	$108.32
MODE OF PAYMENT:	MONTHLY		
ELIMINATION PERIOD:			0 DAYS
CONVALESCENT CARE BENEFIT:			$60 PER DAY
MAXIMUM BENEFIT PERIOD:			3 YEARS
LIFETIME MAXIMUM BENEFIT AMOUNT:			$98,550.OO
ACCIDENTAL DEATH BENEFIT:			$5,000
AMBULANCE BENEFIT			
MAXIMUM BENEFIT FOR EACH TRIP:			$50
WAIVER OF PREMIUM BENEFIT			
ADDITIONAL PURCHASE OPTION DATES:			
	4/22/94 4/22/00 4/22/06		
	4/22/97 4/22/03		
PRESRIPTION DRUG RIDER			
MAXIMUM BENEFIT PER CALENDER MONTH:			$60 PER MONTH

Policy Schedule: Example - 2

POLICY SCHEDULE

Your Elimination Period: 90 calendar days
Your Maximum Lifetime Benefit: $155,736
Your Maximum Monthly Benefit or MMB: $4,326
Benefits Provided by Your Policy

(Deducted From Your Maximum Lifetime Benefit When Paid Unless Otherwise Indicated in Your Policy Schedule)		
NURSING HOME BENEFITS		
Nursing Home Maximum Monthly Benefit	100% of MMB = $4,326 per month	
Nursing Home Bed Reservation Benefit	100% of MMB = $144 per day, up to 30 days in a calendar year	
HOME HEALTH CARE BENEFITS		
Home Health Care Maximum Monthly Benefit	100% of MMB = $4,326 per month	
OTHER BENEFITS INCLUDED IN YOUR COVERAGE		**Your Premium**
Cash Benefit - 40% of Home Health Care Maximum Monthly Benefit = $1,730 per month	Included	Basic Policy
OTHER POLICY BENEFITS		
Respite Care Maximum Monthly Benefit	Pays up to 100% of MMB for one month in a calendar year = $4,326	
Hospice Care Benefit	Pays Nursing Home Benefits and Home Health Care Benefits for Hospice Care	
International Benefit	Pays up to 100% of MMB up to an International Benefit Lifetime Maximum of 12 months = $51,912	
Waiver of Premium	Included	
CARE COORDINATOR BENEFITS		
Care Coordinator Benefit	*THIS BENEFIT IS NOT DEDUCTED FROM YOUR POLICY'S MAXIMUM LIFETIME BENEFIT.*	
Alternate Care Benefit	As approved by your Care Coordinator; subject to your policy's Maximum Lifetime Benefit	
STAY-AT-HOME BENEFITS (AVAILABLE WHEN YOU USE THE CARE COORDINATOR)		
Caregiver Training Benefit	These benefits combined are payable up to your Stay-At-Home Maximum Lifetime Benefit of 2 times the HHC MMB = $8,652	
Durable Medical Equipment Benefit		
Home Modification Benefit		
Medical Alert System Benefit		

OTHER BENEFITS INCLUDED IN YOUR COVERAGE		Your Premium
Compound Inflation Protection With Buy-Up Option 3% Final Buy Up Date Age 85	Included - Buy Up Effective on Schedule Effective Date	$ 705.75
Contingent Nonforfeiture Benefit	Included	Basic Policy
Rate Guarantee Period	5 Years	Basic Policy
BASIC POLICY PREMIUM		$ 855.21
ANNUAL TOTAL PREMIUM (BASIC POLICY + OTHER BENEFITS)		$1,560.96
PREMIUM MODE		Annual
YOUR TOTAL POLICY MODAL PREMIUM		$1,560.96

IF YOU ELECT TO PAY PREMIUMS OTHER THAN ANNUALLY, THE TOTAL AMOUNT OF PREMIUMS YOU WILL PAY EACH YEAR WILL BE GREATER THAN THE ANNUAL PREMIUM SHOWN IN THE TABLE BECAUSE THE COSTS ASSOCIATED WITH ADMINISTERING YOUR POLICY WILL BE GREATER.

Tax Qualified

The policy is intended to be a tax qualified long-term care insurance contract under §7702B(b) of the Internal Revenue Code of 1986, as amended. For additional information concerning the tax status of premiums paid and benefits received under the policy, you should consult your professional tax advisor.

2) The Definitions:

This is possibly the most boring part of the policy, but it is crucial you understand that it is part of the entire contract and use it as you decipher the rest of the contract. For instance, if you find that the contract will trigger with 2 of 6 Activities of Daily Living (ADL's) and it lists them out for you, you will still need to refer to the definitions section to know precisely how the policy defines these activities. Take for example "feeding." While this seems self-evident to the average person, remember this is contract law. If the contract says that "feeding" is the "ability to get food to the mouth while standing on one leg on the carpet" (to use something ludicrous and not anything like what you would see in a contract), then for the purpose of triggering a claim, you must use that definition as the standard. Most of the time, I find people think "feeding" means the ability to shop for food, prepare food, eat, and clean up afterward. However, you should not assume this is what is meant – indeed in most contracts it does NOT mean that! In most contracts, "feeding" simply means can you get food from the plate to your face using a utensil. At the risk of painful reiteration, check the definition in the definitions section. What is written there will be the standard by which the carrier will judge claim eligibility.

3) *Medical triggers and types of care:*

Every claim has 2 things that must be "met" for the claim to be approved: health triggers and type of care triggers. And let us be clear this is an "AND" provision in contract law. BOTH of these things must match the contract language for a claim to be approved. If a claimant only matches one of the two, then the claim may still be denied. Let us look at each:

> ***NOTE BENE:*** Contracts require policy owners meet BOTH the medical triggers and type-of-care trigger. This is an AND provision in the contract.

Medical Triggers: This is one of the more misunderstood parts of long term care contracts by the uninitiated. People who are not familiar with contract law somehow believe that just because they WANT something to be true about an insurance policy, it SHOULD be true. They are notably upset when the contract indeed becomes the level ground to which everyone's expectations must return. A case in point is macular degeneration. Let us imagine Parent is now legally blind from this condition and has recently moved to an ALF. Dutiful thinks the long term care policy should now pay for care. The answer is that it may... or it may not. Though Parent is clearly in a long term care environment, we would have to carefully read the contract to know if a claim was likely or if we are premature in filing. An older policy that has "fuzzier" language and looser definitions of medical need for care might allow payment. More modern policies that have more precise language might not. This is the case of "just because it is in the garage, it isn't necessarily a car" problem – just because a person is receiving care services, it doesn't mean she is claim eligible.

We again run upon the rocky shoals of the wide variation on contracts over the 30+ years of evolution in this industry. In general, if you find policies written post 1996,[6] they will be tax-qualified and have standardized triggers for claims.[7] Policies prior to that will not be very standardized. Finally, and the thing that most often

---

6 The Kennedy / Kasselbaum welfare and health care reform legislation was signed into law in August 1996 and became effective January of 1997 http://www.prepsmart.com/tax-qualified-ltci-policies.html. Prep Smart, Long term care answers.

7 And – to be clear – even after 1996, there are still non-Tax Qualified policies sold in the market where the medical triggers for claim may have wide variation.

makes people angry, very few contracts list medicine management or driving as triggers. So there is simply no substitute for reading the contract and knowing the minimum thresholds of medically necessary care that will trigger a claim. If you have been keeping a spreadsheet or notebook to track details, this is a good detail to note in your budding system.

For simplicity, we will use a Tax Qualified policy as the example in the remainder of this document. The figure below shows the usual contract definition for medically necessary care in a tax qualified policy.

TAX QUALIFIED POLICIES REQUIRE ONE OF THESE TWO TO BE TRUE TO TRIGGER A CLAIM:

2 of 6 Activities of Daily Living:

- Transferring
- Bathing
- Dressing
- Eating
- Continence
- Toileting

OR

Severe Cognitive Impairment that requires supervision.

As simple as that OR equation is in the diagram, there can be complexities. On the Activities of Daily Living (ADLs) for instance, some contracts will require hands-on help, some will allow "stand by" help, and others won't specify at all. If there is specificity, it is usually in the definitions section. Thus, the person reading the contract has to know (1) what the ADL triggers are, (2) how many are required from one section of the contract, and then (3) refer to the definitions section to be certain you know if it will trigger for hands-on, stand-by, or something else.

Measuring the alternate trigger, severe cognitive impairment, is more difficult typically. The problem lies in the poor definition of "severe." Some contracts will specify the use of clinical cognitive screens to measure impairment while other contracts will include a Doctor's clinical observations and diagnosis. Since a person with cognitive impairment will very likely "fail" a cognitive screen, it is usually just easier to have someone administer the screening test than argue over a physician's professional opinion.

There are several cognitive screens, but the most common are the MMSE and the SICS (see definitions at the end of this document for full names). Further, the carrier is looking at how *badly* a Person "failed." If a normal score is 20 out of 30 and your client gets 18 out of 30... is that enough to be severe? Or is it only enough to be mild? Clearly 10 out of 30 gets a severe label. The difference in claim approval or denial on cases that get a middle-of-the-road result is usually what the physician observes in the clinical visit and the information that the family reports to the doctor.

This can be further complicated because many dementia patients do OK when they are rested, but as the day progresses and they tire or their blood sugar drops before lunch (or other factors), their ability wanes. So the same patient taking the same clinical test might score 18 in the morning but drop to 12 by midafternoon. Thus, the doctor's recommendation as to the severity of the cognitive impairment as well as his/her recommendation for supervision can often sway a mid-ground case towards or away from claim eligibility. If you know what the contract requires and understand how dementia can vary throughout the day, then you are better armed to get the appropriate tests done (at the right time of day!) and help the doctor understand what documentation to write in the file.

The bottom line on medical triggers: the policy holder must be able to document in medical records that there is a level of care required at this point in his/her life that precision matches the minimum thresholds in the contract. If you cannot document medical need for care and minimum thresholds of care, then filing a claim is premature.

The AND provision now swings around and kicks us squarely in the behind. If we can manage the medical triggers, we still must clear the hurdle of type of care.

Type-of-Care Triggers: If medical triggers are some of the most misunderstood, then the Type-of-Care is the second most. So often family members are angry because Parent has paid on this policy for 20 years and it will only pay for a nursing home?!?! [Do please hear the outrage and indignation in the vocal tone – this is a sure sign someone hasn't read the contract carefully.] Humans suffer from a disease we call "WANT IT TO" sickness. They want the policy to pay for home health care and so they are horrified to learn it will not. Or they wanted to "save the policy for when Mom really needed it" and, at the threshold of assisted living, learn the policy was home care only. This is where "WANT IT TO" sickness can get us into real trouble. Since we have "wanted" reality to be this for so long, we have trouble accepting where we are at now – having waited too long to read and understand the contract. The sad truth is that no lawyer or other professional you appeal to can modify the contract to match the "want it to."

So, where do we find this illusive information? Somewhere in the contract (or a rider – see the section on riders below) it will lay out in very clear language what type of care will be paid for and what type will not. The broad categories are: home health care (HHC), assisted living facility (ALF), adult day care (ADC), and nursing home (NH). These are generally defined by a state license and/or criteria (laid out in high levels of detail!) about types of nurses on staff, hours on duty and on call, and types of services provided. I find most states will license the ADC, ALF and NH. Many states, however, do not license HHC. This can be a sticky-wicket if a family wants to have a neighbor provide the care for Dad in his home, but the policy requires a licensed HHC provider. As always, the contract is the final authority and if it requires a license by the state, then the neighbor can be hired to provide the care... but the policy won't pay for it. Read the contract carefully, however... if it doesn't require a state licensure, sometimes a local business license will suffice to fill the bill. The details and precise language used in the contract can make or break this part of the claim.

Those vocabulary, however, are more modern. If you have an older contract, you may see it uses other language such as "skilled care, intermediate care, or custodial care." Or you may see it speaks of "medical care and non-medical care." We have even seen "professional care and non-professional." Let us pause just a moment and give you some general equivalencies among these various types of descriptions. The table below lays out how – usually - carriers will cross-walk old language to the modern care field. However, be advised that this is "usually." It is always wise to call the carrier to confirm that this is how they will interpret.

Nursing Home	Assisted Living
• Skilled care • Medical care • Professional (meaning RN, LPN, therapist or doctor)	• Intermediate Care • Custodial Care • Non-professional • Non-medical care • House-keeping services
Adult Day Care	**Home Health Care**
• Custodial • Non-professional • Non-medical	• This can run the entire gamut of types of care. Any of the vocabulary MAY apply here

One last note about old and new vocabulary problems: there may be items that will end up being "shades of grey" and can benefit from a well-written justification. A case we filed a few years ago had a contract stating it would not pay in a "boarding house" and yet the state where the client lived licensed the ALF as a dual entity. The license stated clearly that it was "A boarding house and assisted living facility." The policy clearly would pay an ALF but not a boarding house. So it took some creativity on our part to pull legal statutes from the state to indicate that "boarding house" was a vestigial name and that the community in question was truly an ALF. Some fast tap-dancing there allowed the claim to be approved. So don't hesitate in grey areas to launch a logical argument. You will win some and lose some - but you can't win any if you don't try.

In conclusion, a person seeking to file a claim needs to be able to meet both the medical triggers in the policy AND be receiving care from a provider that will meet the type-of-care definitions in the policy. All of this will require documentation (lots of it) - remember the Fairytale we started with? We weren't just telling you a tall tale...

4) *Claim procedures*

Some contracts (more typical of the more modern ones) will lay out procedures for claim. Often these procedures have time windows listed as to how quickly you must notify the carrier of a claim after loss (usually it will say a 90 day window if it gives this detail – though we have seen some with 180 day window) and/or how quickly all documentation must be submitted for a claim to be considered. These are crucial because – by contract – the carrier could deny a claim if it is submitted beyond the window or if only part of the required documentation arrives on time.

I have seen very few carriers that were unwilling to work with families, though. Often the need for claim is in a time of crisis and the crisis is so severe that the actual filing of a claim gets delayed. So even if you are beyond the window in the contract, don't hesitate to ask for leniency and plead "extenuating circumstances" as you have a good chance of garnering it. If, however, you try to back file a year or more on care expenses, it is wise to examine the contract limitations on claim filing.

5) *Any riders or modifiers*

Finally – but certainly not least – you are looking to see if there are any riders or contract modifiers.

- Riders: usually these were purchased with the policy and will be attached at the back of the overall contract. Older policies, for instance, will often be a facility only contract, but then have a home health care rider. The rider is always resting on top of the original contract – when a rider does not specify a change, the original contract holds authority. For instance, if I have a contract with a home health care rider that says nothing about the elimination period (the deductible window), then whatever deductible was in the original contract is still the correct number. However, if that same contract says that home care deductible is at zero days where the original contract is at 90 days, then what we have is a policy that will pay upon the first day for home health care, but has a 90 day self-pay window for facility because the rider lays on top of or "overrides" the original contract. These are but two examples – there can be many variations in riders. Just remember that the rider modifies the existing contract. If there is an issue on which the rider doesn't comment, then the original contract still holds the correct provision.

> ***NOTE BENE:*** Riders modify the original contract. If the rider has no mention of an item (say a deductible) then the original contract holds authority.

- Other modifiers: more commonly than people realize, policy owners may have signed letters of modification to their original contract. Time and again we find a policy that shows X provision (say a zero day elimination period) and when it finally pays, the carrier says they have Y benefit (say a 90 day elimination period). Why this discrepancy? Because 15 years into ownership, the policy owner decided the premiums were too high (or had some other reason!) and opted to drop the benefits back or change a feature. They signed the required documentation, sent it to the carrier, and now the policy is different than originally issued. Most of the time, the policy owner doesn't remember having done this and no one kept up with the documentation - but the carrier did. So know that you can (and often will) run into modifying agreements from the original contract. Be sure you check with the carrier to know what modifiers are on file.

Summary on Reading The Contract

Read the contract. I know, I know! How self-evident is that by this point? I state it again because all too often folks want (long for, look for, and attempt!) shortcuts. Reading the contract IS the shortcut. There is no guessing game that can be played here. Someone has to both read the contract and understand how the various parts fit together (i.e. how the definitions section can inform that triggers listed OR how the rider is modifying the original contract OR...).

Since these are complicated beasties, taking a few notes never hurts. As we said earlier, a spreadsheet that lists the items, values, and notes never hurts either.

If you think "Whew! That is a lot of information to keep up with" – welcome to the world of claims. It is a lot. Reading and understanding the contract are just the beginning salvos – if it appears that a claim is probable, someone now has to file it. As we illustrated with the fairytale that we opened with, the process can be fraught with many pitfalls and perils. To avoid The Highly Stressful Situation that Dutiful demonstrated, we recommend one simple solution: someone wrangle the claim.

Notice we said "someone" – not multiple people, but just ONE person. As we will explain in the next section, it is far too easy for the left hand to not know what the right hand is doing. If there isn't a central figure managing (we call it "quarterbacking") the process, there is much chance for failure.

THIS was what Dutiful was facing (as you no doubt recall):

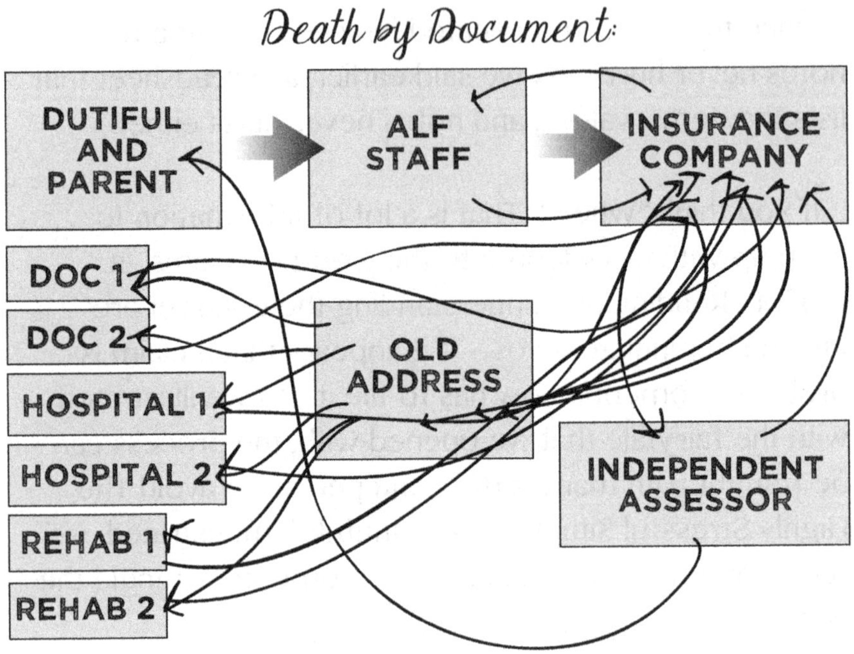

This monolithic nightmare can be tamed to a much more manageable process if Dutiful will don the mantel of "Quarterback" and start calling the shots on the field.

When Dutiful (or someone) takes on this mantel, the process would look more like the following:

A More Successful Process:

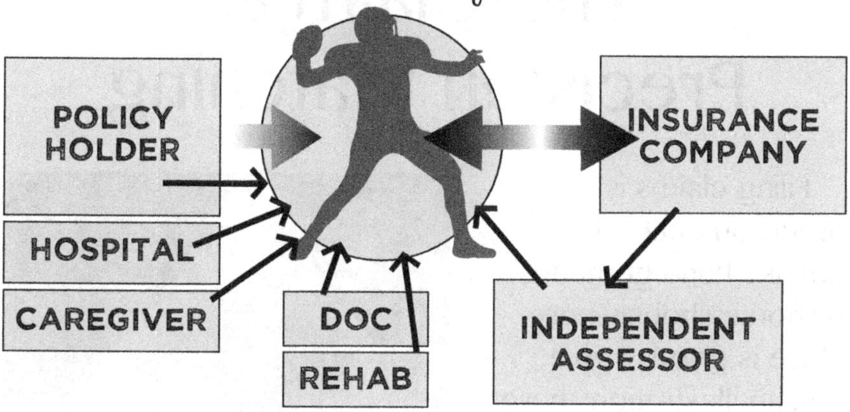

We confess that it is still an unwieldy process. There are still multiple forms being faxed or mailed around, phone calls being made to follow up and make sure all the pages of the fax got in the right file, and other such verification bits. But at least in this paradigm, SOMEONE has a hand on the process and is managing it just as the Nice Lady and Her Minions do in the Doctor's office. This person may be Dutiful him/herself. More often, people will elect to hire a professional to do this for them (just like the doctor has professionals who do it for him/her!).

The importance of the Quarterback's job is not just to make sure everything is going round to the various cubby holes as it should, but also to make sure that all the documents say what they need to say and that they match the contract – which was the purpose of reading the contract in the first place, after all. So let us turn our attention now to the more delicate business of precision document matching.

The Claim & Precision Matching

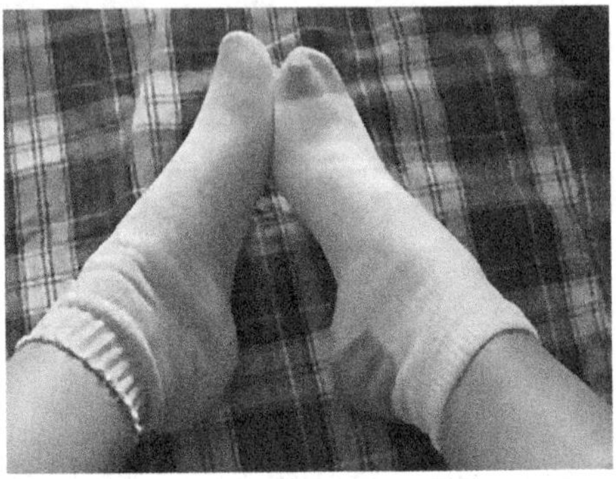

Filing claims is a precision deal – it is not like hand grenades or horse shoes where close is good. I give you an illustration: here is a picture of my son's socks. Now, in all fairness at the time of the photo, my son was 20 years old, lived alone, and was going to college on a budget.

So I look at this matching job and think, "Well, at least they are both white...-ish." This is how most people approach the documentation requirements for the long term care claim: "-ish". "-Ish" may work some of the time – in fact folks who get through on "-ish" documentation probably have no idea that they squeaked by – but folks who get a denial of claim become keenly aware that "ish" is a risky place to stand if you are relying on the money from the policy to bail you out of a tight financial spot (as most families are). So let's look at some examples of how "ish" matching can catch us unawares.

As you recall, we must match TWO items:

1) Medical need for care and

2) Where the care is provided

Let's say we have a tax-qualified policy that has this standardized definition of medically necessary care to trigger (see box below): *transferring, bathing, dressing, eating, toileting, and continence. Careful reading of the contract indicates that the client needs stand-by level of assistance on 2 of the 6 to qualify.*

Further we discover that it will only pay in a facility that meets these requirements: *A facility, other than a hospital, which is primarily engaged in providing nursing care on an inpatient basis under a license issued by the appropriate licensing agency. It may be freestanding facility, including skilled nursing homes, intermediate care homes, intermediate personal care homes, one-bed adult day care homes or it may be a distinct part of a facility, including a ward, wing or unit or a swing-bed of a hospital or other institution.*

POLICY REQUIRES
2 OF 6 DAILY LIVING ACTIVITIES
TO TRIGGER.

- Transferring
- Bathing
- Continence
- Dressing
- Eating
- Toileting

This is the scenario: Dutiful has been hiring home health care help for Parent and has finally decided the financials are at a place where they need to trigger the policy. Will the policy pay? Well first off, we can rule out home health care because the definition for the type of care provide says "facility" the first rattle out of the box.

Even in gross matching terms, this contract will not pay home health care. So Dutiful starts shopping assisted living facilities. Will the policy pay there? Answer: yes, so long as they are properly licensed since "intermediate care" is usually equivalent to ALF level care. As long as we can prove the appropriate licensure, we are good on this part. Now the truly tricky business kicks in...

You must be able to provide documents that indicate Parent has medical need for 2 of the 6 ADLs. Further you must be able to provide this proof from both the care provider (the ALF) and the primary doctor.

Here (if you were god-like and could see them with your x-ray vision) are the things you might see:

The Family: Mom has a high fall risk. She uses a walker and needs someone in the room when bathing in case she falls. She is able to dress herself except for socks and shoes, which she needs some help with. She needs medication reminders and wears adult diapers due to incontinence.

The ALF Assessment: They will give medication reminders, provide stand-by assistance for showering, and will do light housekeeping and meal preparation for her.

The Doctor's notes: She needs help with medications, is incontinent and wearing adult diapers, she is a high fall risk with fragile bones and requires supervision while showering and transferring in case of a fall.

This is a classic "-ish" situation. According to the family, we have 3 of the 6 (bathing, dressing, and incontinence). Clearly this would be a claim approved if this were the only document. However, the ALF records only indicate 1of 6 (stand-by assistance for showering) - the other items shown in the ALF records would be paid for by the policy -- but they are not sufficient to <u>trigger</u> the policy. One of the biggest misunderstandings is that just because someone needs help with medications doesn't mean the policy will pay because medication reminders are not usually a trigger for the policy (even though most of us wish they were). Finally, the doctor's notes indicate 3 of 6 (incontinence, showering and transferring). The bigger problem is that none of these match each other and at least one (the ALF) doesn't match the policy. These inconsistencies can cause carriers to wonder if there is fraud going on and/or if they have an inaccurate picture of what is happening and, therefore, they can't make a claim determination. If each of these is sent in independently - say without a quarterback to review the documents before they go in - then we are into matching "-ish" land and you may or may not get a claim approved.

This same precision matching issue is true when you trigger on cognitive impairment - though to a lesser degree. Cognitive impairment is judged by failure to perform within normal range on standardized tests. Since the scales for "normal" on these tests are well established, usually if the doctor's notes (1) indicate the test score(s) and (2) remarks that the patient needs supervision, the case will be approved for claim. This would be true even if the policy holder is not in a special "memory care" unit or has no ADLs listed in the documents from the care provider. The simple fact that the doctor wrote 'needs supervision' or 'cannot live alone' renders the need for care self-evident. In this case you only have to have documentation that the care provider matches the policy definition for approved care. To be clear, however, the doctor must indicate BOTH (1) and (2) -- that is (1) "moderate" or "severe" cognitive impairment AND (2) "requires supervision." If you only get one of these two in the doctor's recommendation or notes, then you are back into "-ish" territory. (Please note - earlier in the document we discussed the finer points of gauging "severe," "moderate," and "mild" levels of dementia... all of that is still relevant here).

One parting shot about precision matching in claims - always, but **always** match the contract. The examples I have given here are from newer, tax-qualified policies that have standardized triggers. If you are working with an older policy or one that is not tax-qualified, you can find the definitions can vary quite widely.

Here is a good example:

> The insured person must need care designed essentially to help a person in the activities of daily living and which does not require the continuous attention of trained medical or paramedical personnel. Such care may involve (1) the preparation of special diets; (2) supervision over medication that can be self-administered; and (3) assistance in getting in and out of bed, walking, bathing, dressing, and eating.

On this policy, documentation indicating the person is diabetic and needs special meal preparation (or low salt intake due to heart problems or.) and cannot drive or prep food him/herself would meet the trigger. To be safe, a person filing the claim should also document every other part of the care requirements that can be documented to insure we are not only at the minimum threshold to trigger but well beyond the line of doubt. So if you could document a diabetic diet requirement along with inability to drive/shop and that the person had to have stand-by help when showering due to high fall risk, you would be beyond the doubt territory. And if you could add another piece about needing to be reminded to check blood sugars and administer insulin or take a blood pressure pill, you would be well beyond.

Summary on The Claim Process

Well, it isn't rocket science - but it isn't child's play either (to borrow and butcher tired old adages!). Filing a long term care claim requires some patience and the ability to read and track progression of a process that requires a high degree of precision handling of documents and details. A professional who knows what s/he is doing will take an average of 8 to 10 working hours spread across a 3 to 4 week period to get a claim approved (the long window is because you are nearly always waiting on doctor offices and other places to get you the required forms - and if you have to ask them to re-do the form or letter to more precisely match, it extends the time). For a lay person to tackle this task, the estimate is probably at least double because of the learning curve on vocabulary and things that must be done again because they didn't get done right the first time in the learning process.

Sometimes - in a very few instances - we have seen it take no energy or effort on the part of the family to get a claim approved. This is usually when it is a clear cognitive impairment situation and when the carrier in question handles the entire process without asking anything of the family. It would be ideal if it worked this way every time. But it does not - in fact that is the exception rather than the rule. From our perspective, even on the "slam dunk" cases that will approve with little effort, a family is better to have their hand on the claim process just to insure they don't somehow end up in "-ish" land where claims are denied. [8]

---

8 There is sometimes an appeal process if you are denied. There isn't time or room in this document to go into all the ins and outs of an appeal. Some carriers will let you start anew with a new claim – though most carriers have a file on a claimant and the file never disappears. If you are denied this year and then next year health is worse so you now want to reapply for claim, there isn't a new claim – you are just modifying the old claim. This is why – in the general scheme of things – it is FAR FAR easier to do it right the first time than try to appeal or apply again later... because in any appeal or later claim, you are working against the earlier documentation already on file.

Conclusion: Where to From Here?

You've read all the way to the end. So now what?

Well, now you get started:

- Read the contract
- Start a Contact Log
- Follow up consistently

The shortest route to success is to hire a professional to do this for you (unless you are a professional reading this!). If you are going to be the quarterback and (wo)man-handle this yourself, then it is time to put on your Prince(ss) Dutiful Garb and start making some phone calls, open a contact log, file your DPOA and authorizations with all the players at the table (carrier, doctor's office, hospital, rehab, HHC, ALF or NH provider), start pulling the required documents and make sure they are filled out in a way that precision matches the contract. Get everything faxed to the carrier and call the carrier. And call some more to be sure the faxes arrived in their entirety and see if they need any other documentation. Pull that documentation – be sure it matches. Fax to the carrier. Call the carrier to see if it arrived in its entirety. Find out if there is anything still outstanding, if there is you pull THOSE documents, make sure it matches the contract, fax to the carrier... call the carrier... and you ride the merry-go-round until you get an answer that says "claim approved" – then you are on semi-easy street where you only have to mount the merry-go-round as you manage the monthly claims and any future re-assessments.

If your head is swimming, I know and understand. We have filed claims for policy holders here at Mrs. LTC, Inc. long enough to have the merry-go-round pattern down to a fine art. Believe me when I say this: when you have a claim approved and paying, it will have been worth every circle round the way...

If we can ever be of help, you can find us at:

www.MrsLTC.com

Best wishes for a good ride!

Appendix

Definitions:

ACTIVITIES OF DAILY LIVING (ADLS): Everyday functions and activities individuals usually do without help. ADL functions include bathing, continence, dressing, eating, toileting and transferring. Many policies use the inability to do a certain number of ADLS (such as 2 of 6) to decide when a policy holder is claim eligible.

ADULT DAY CARE (ADC): Care provided during the day at a community-based center for adults who need assistance of supervision during the day including help with personal care. Typically people utilize adult day care services when family are doing evening and weekend care, but family have to work and the person needs a place to go during care givers are at work.

ALTERNATE PLAN OF CARE: This is an option found in some policies that indicates when the carrier might consider some type of care other than what is listed as the primary type of care the policy will cover. One example might be that it allows for payment in an ALF when the contract was written for a NH. The exact language of these has varied over the years, so there is no way to give an all-inclusive definition of what it might provide. A careful reading of the contract will let you know what and when this provision may be considered for payment of benefits.

ASSISTED LIVING (ALF): A residential living arrangement that provides individualized personal care and health services for people who require assistance with ADLs. The types and sized of facilities may vary; they can range from a small 3 or 4 bedroom home to a large apartment-style complex. They also vary in the levels of care and services provided. ALFs offer a way to keep a relatively independent lifestyle for people who don't need the level of care provide in skilled care or in nursing home environments.

BED RESERVATION: Some policies provide a benefit that allows the payment of claim for a room or bed in an ALF or NH when the client has had to have a temporary stay in a hospital or rehab unit. There is typically a limit on the number of days per year that is covered under this benefit.

BENEFIT AMOUNT: The sum of money paid to a claimant for which the insurance company has received the premiums. It is usually listed as a daily, monthly, or weekly amount.

COGNITIVE IMPAIRMENT: A deficiency in a person's short or long term memory; orientation as to person, time or place; deductive or abstract reasoning; judgment as it relates to safety and awareness. Contracts can specify that a person must be "moderate" or "severe" in their impairment to trigger claim payments. The level of severity is almost always measured and documented by standardized clinical tests administered by doctors, nurses, or social workers.

ELIMINATION PERIOD: This is essentially the deductible and can sometimes be called a "wait window." It is specified as a number of days that a claimant must pay 100% of the cost of care before the carrier will begin to paying. Policies will only pay benefits when a claimant receives eligible services. It is wise to know if your elimination period is in terms of "calendar days" or "service days" and to note if any days paid by Medicare or other insurance will count towards these deductible days.

HANDS-ON ASSISTANCE: Physical assistance (minimal, moderate, or maximal) without which the individual would not be able to perform the ADL. Typically, a care provide must put "hands on" the client in order for the action (like getting out of bed or showering) to be performed.

HOME HEALTH CARE (HHC): Services for nursing care or occupational, physical, respiratory, or speech therapy. Also included are medical, social worker, home health aide, and homemaker services.

INFLATION RIDER (INFLATION GROWTH): an option you can add to a basic policy that will increase the benefit levels to help pay for the expected increases in the cost of care between when you buy the policy and when you expect to use it.

MEDICATION MANAGEMENT: This service can range from simple reminders to self-administer medication all the way up thru a licensed care provider (usually a nurse) who can measure and deliver medications.

MINI-MENTAL STATE EXAM (MMSE): also known as the **Folstein Test**, it is a brief 30-point questionnaire that is used to screen for cognitive impairment. It is also used to estimate the severity of cognitive impairment and to follow the course of cognitive changes in an individual over time, thus making it an effective way to document an individual's response to treatment.

NURSING HOME (NH): a licensed facility that provides general nursing care to shoe who are chronically ill or unable to take care of daily living needs. May also be called a long term care facility and is sometimes an extension of a hospital or rehabilitation unit.

POOL OF MONEY: Some policies operate as a clock where you have a finite time limit to use the benefits. However, policies that operate from a pool of money indicate that there is a maximum amount of money available in the policy. The policy will continue to pay benefits until the entire pool is gone. Typically the pool is calculated by multiplying the daily benefit (or monthly) by the time multiplier. So a $3000/month benefit with a 3 year multiplier would calculate the pool as this: $3,000 X 3years = $108,000 pool of money.

REDUCTION FOR ALF OR HHC: Some policies have the capacity to reduce the daily or monthly benefit amount by a percentage amount. For instance, a policy may have $5000/month for facility based care but have a 50% reduction for home care (HHC). In this example, the client would have $2500/month available for home care but $5000 for facility care.

RESPITE CARE: Care provided by a third part that relieves family caregivers for a few hours to several days and gives them an occasional break from daily caregiving responsibilities.

RESTORATION: Some policies will have a restoration rider added to them. This rider means that if a person uses the policy for a round of care - and doesn't use the policy completely up - and gets better, then the carrier will top the pool of money up to its original amount for the next time the owner needs to use the policy. The most common usage of this type of rider is if someone has cancer or an accident that requires long windows of care for the recovery period.

RIDER: An addition to an insurance policy that changes the provisions in the policy. Usually the rider has authority when there is a discrepancy between the original contract and the rider. However if the rider doesn't address some portion of content from the original contract, the original contract holds the authority (i.e. if HHC rider allows for payment of care at home, but doesn't mention the elimination period at all, then the original contract's definition of the elimination period will apply to the HHC benefits).

RX BENEFIT: This is more typical in older polices. You will occasionally find that there is a small reimbursable amount for expenditures on doctor prescribed medications.

SHARED CARE: A rider that allows two people to merge their pools of money. If the first person who needs care drinks his/her pool of money dry and still needs care, s/he has the option of drinking from the other person's pool. Or, conversely, if the first person dies with money still in his/her bucket, the surviving person inherits what is left in that bucket to use for care.

SIX-ITEM SCREENER (SIS OR SCIS): One of the two most common standardized tests to measure cognitive impairment (the other is called the Mini-Mental State Exam or MMSE).

STAND-BY ASSISTANCE: A level of assistance where a care giver doesn't necessarily put hands on the client to offer help, but rather is standing near-by in case the client needs help to finish the ADL or appears to be in danger of injury (for instance, a person may get out of a chair well most of the time but now and then has a balance issue that could result in a fall).

STAY AT HOME BENEFIT (HOME MODIFICATION): This is typical of more modern policies. They offer a small sum of money to pay for home modification or durable medical equipment so that a claimant has a chance of staying in home care longer.

SURVIVORSHIP: A rider offered with some policies purchased by couples. The rider typical is not effective until the policy has been owner for a window of time with no claims (usually 10 years). Once the window has been met, the rider provides that the surviving spouse's premiums are paid-in full up on the death of the first spouse.

TAX-QUALIFIED: A policy that confirms to certain standards in federal law and offers some federal tax advantages. As of the writing of this document, the primary advantage was that the benefits paid for care were not taxable as income once they were paid. However, this law can be changed at any time and so it is always wise to consult with a tax professional if this is a concern.

TIME WINDOW: nearly every policy will designate a time window for how long the policy will pay benefits. Some older policies may show that this is "unlimited," meaning the policy would pay until the claimant passes away. Newer policies all have time limits on them and will be noted in terms of days or years. It is important to read the contract to know if this time window is a clock or if it is a multiplier to calculate the Pool of Money.

WAIVER OF HOME HEALTH CARE (WAIVER OF HHC): A rider found in some policies that says the elimination period is waived when the claim starts as home health care.

WAIVER OF PREMIUM: a provision in the policy that relieves the insured of paying the premiums while receiving benefits.

Made in the USA
Monee, IL
11 November 2026

68342120R00036